by Stuart Schwartz and Craig Conley

Consultant:
Robert J. Miller, Ph.D.
Professor of Special Education
Mankato State University

CAPSTONE
HIGH/LOW BOOKS
an imprint of Capstone Press
Mankato, Minnesota

Capstone High/Low Books are published by Capstone Press
818 North Willow Street • Mankato, MN 56001
http://www.capstone-press.com

Library of Congress Cataloging-in-Publication Data
Schwartz, Stuart, 1945–
    Buying insurance/by Stuart Schwartz and Craig Conley.
    p. cm. — (Life skills)
    Includes bibliographical references and index.
    Summary: Explains the different kinds of insurance, including automobile, health, disability, life, homeowner's, and renter's, discusses how to choose which type to buy, and provides advice on choosing an insurance agent.
    ISBN 0-7368-0045-X
    1. Insurance—Juvenile literature. [1. Insurance.] I. Conley, Craig, 1965- .
II. Title. III. Series: Schwartz, Stuart, 1945–   Life skills.
HG8052.5.S39   1999
368—dc21   98-35116
                                                     CIP
                                                     AC

Editorial Credits

Christy Steele, editor; James Franklin, cover designer and illustrator; Michelle L.
  Norstad, photo researcher

Photo credits

All photographs by Barb Stitzer Photography

Table of Contents

Chapter 1

Insurance

People buy insurance to protect themselves in case of unexpected expenses. Insurance is a contract between a person and an insurance company. The person pays money to an insurance company. In exchange, the insurance company agrees to pay some or all of the person's unexpected expenses. Unexpected expenses can come from events such as car accidents or floods.

People receive policies when they buy insurance. Policies describe the agreements between people and their insurance companies.

Each policy describes coverage. Coverage is the expenses the insurance company agrees to pay. A policy also lists the requirements for receiving payment for the expenses. People should read their policies carefully. They should ask questions if they do not understand their policies.

People can buy insurance to protect almost anything. Some people even buy insurance for their pets. People should think about which items they would like to protect with insurance.

Some people buy insurance for their pets.

Chapter 2

Automobile Insurance

Automobile insurance provides coverage for unexpected automobile expenses. Automobile insurance policies list information about the insurance people buy.

Every car owner must buy liability insurance. A liability is something a person is responsible for under law. People need liability insurance in case they cause an accident. Their insurance then will pay most of the expenses of any accident victims. Car owners need this protection in case someone sues them for damages they cause.

Some states require people to buy no-fault insurance. No-fault coverage protects the car owner no matter who causes an accident. The insurance company pays the policy holders for any expenses.

Many people buy other types of insurance too. Collision insurance covers car repairs for damage caused by accidents. Comprehensive insurance covers other kinds of damages such as car theft or dents left by hail.

Automobile insurance provides coverage for unexpected automobile expenses.

Chapter 3

Automobile Insurance Coverage

People can choose to buy different types of automobile insurance coverage. People choose the amount of coverage they want to buy. The car owners must pay any expenses over the amount of coverage they have purchased.

Personal injury coverage protects a person from medical expenses due to accidents. The insurance company pays part or all of the hospital costs. It also pays funeral costs if the person dies.

Property damage coverage is automobile insurance that pays for damage to property. For example, the insurance company pays if a driver damages fences, lawns, or houses.

The cost of an automobile insurance policy depends on the kinds of insurance and coverage a person buys. The cost also depends on the value of a person's car. Expensive cars cost more to insure than inexpensive cars. An insurance company must pay more to replace or repair expensive cars.

Expensive cars cost more to insure than inexpensive cars.

Chapter 4

Health Insurance

Health insurance covers part or all of a person's doctor, hospital, and medicine bills. For example, a hospital stay may cost several hundred dollars per day. Insurance helps people pay for the care they need.

Many people have two kinds of health insurance. Basic medical insurance covers doctor bills and hospital bills. It also covers surgical bills when a person needs an operation. It pays for hospital care and treatment such as medical tests and medicine.

Major medical insurance is another type of health insurance. It pays for large expenses that basic medical insurance does not cover. It pays for extended hospital stays and certain treatments.

Some people buy individual health insurance. Others buy health insurance as part of a group. Most large companies offer health insurance for their employees. Workers usually pay part of their medical costs. This is called a co-payment. Companies pay for the insurance policies.

Health insurance covers part or all of people's doctor, hospital, and medicine costs.

Chapter 6

Life Insurance

Some people buy life insurance. Life insurance pays money to a beneficiary when a policy holder dies. The policy holder chooses a beneficiary to receive benefits from the life insurance policy.

There are two kinds of life insurance. Term life insurance covers a person for a certain length of time. For example, a term life insurance policy might cover 10 years of a person's lifetime. That person would need to buy a new policy after the 10-year period ends.

Whole life insurance covers a person until the person dies. Whole life insurance is more expensive than term life insurance.

Many people buy life insurance to support their families or friends. Parents may want to leave money to their children. People may want to leave money to help their families pay for funerals.

People buy life insurance to support their families.

Chapter 7

Homeowner's Insurance

People who own houses need homeowner's insurance. Homeowner's insurance policies pay part of the costs for damaged homes.

Homeowner's insurance also covers the contents of a house. The insurance company will pay to replace any stolen items. It also will replace belongings damaged in a fire or a storm.

Homeowner's insurance also covers personal liability. A homeowner is responsible for visitors' safety. The homeowner might be sued if people fall and hurt themselves.

Insurance companies will not pay to replace possessions unless people can prove the value of these items. People should keep records of what they own. They should write down the model numbers and the serial numbers of their possessions. They also should take photographs of each room. They then will be able to ask for the proper amount from their insurance company. People should keep these records in a safe place.

People should take photographs of each room to prove the value of their possessions.

Chapter 8

Renter's Insurance

People who rent houses or apartments can buy renter's insurance. Renter's insurance covers a renter's belongings. The insurance company will pay to repair or replace damaged items.

Renter's insurance does not cover damage to a renter's building or apartment. The renter must take care of walls, carpets, or cabinets. Renters have to pay for any damage they cause to their apartments.

Renters should keep a record of their possessions just as home owners do. They should take photographs of their property. Renters should write down the model and serial numbers of their possessions.

Renters should write down the model and serial numbers of their possessions.

Chapter 9

Getting Quotes

It is important to be a careful shopper for insurance. People will receive better protection if they shop carefully. They also can save money by shopping for the best deal.

People find the best insurance deals by getting quotes from many insurance companies. A quote gives them the estimated price that insurance companies charge for different policies.

People should ask insurance agents for copies of the policies they are interested in purchasing. They should read each policy carefully and compare what each one offers. People should choose the best policy for the least money.

People find the best insurance deals by getting quotes from many insurance companies.

Chapter 10

Deductibles

People should find out how much the deductible is on each policy. A deductible is the amount of expenses a policy holder must pay before the insurance pays anything.

People can choose the amount of their deductibles. For example, a person might choose to have a $500 deductible. That means they must pay the first $500 if they have an accident, become ill, or have property damage. The insurance company pays the remaining costs.

People should compare the deductibles of different policies. They should decide on the amount of deductible they can afford. Policies with high deductibles cost less than policies with low deductibles. People with high deductibles pay less for their insurance because the insurance company's risk is lower. Insurance companies do not have to pay as much in damages to policy holders with high deductibles.

People should decide what deductible they can afford.

Chapter 11

Choosing an Insurance Company

Insurance agents can answer people's questions. Agents can help people decide what kinds of insurance they need. People should choose an insurance company with helpful insurance agents who answer questions honestly.

People need to talk with agents to see which insurance companies meet their needs. People should look for a company that has been in business for a long time. People also can check with the Better Business Bureau to make sure the insurance company is honest.

People should choose insurance companies with helpful agents.

Chapter 12

Meeting Insurance Needs

People should know what kind of coverage they need. They then should make sure insurance policies meet their needs before buying them. They should read policies carefully and know what the insurance covers. People should understand the advantages and disadvantages of each kind of insurance.

People must decide what type of insurance policies they can afford. Their insurance companies will send bills for the insurance. The amounts people pay are called premiums. It is important to pay insurance premiums on time. Insurance companies may cancel policies if payments are late.

People who have a good safety record receive lower insurance premiums than those who do not. For example, safe drivers often receive lower insurance rates than unsafe drivers. An insurance company may raise the insurance rates of people who have had car accidents or speeding tickets.

It is important to pay insurance premiums on time.

Words to Know

beneficiary (ben-uh-FISH-uhr-ee)—a person who receives benefits from a life insurance policy

benefit (BEN-uh-fit)—a service an insurance company provides

coverage (KUHV-rij)—the expenses that an insurance company agrees to pay

deductible (di-DUHK-tuh-buhl)—an expense a policy holder must pay

insurance (in-SHU-ruhnss)—a contract between a person and an insurance company

liability (lye-uh-BI-luh-tee)—something a person is responsible for under law

policy (POL-uh-see)—a written agreement between a person and an insurance company

premium (PREE-mee-uhm)—the amount a person pays for insurance

quote (KWOTE)—an estimated price for insurance

To Learn More

Enteen, Robert. *Health Insurance: How to Get It, Keep It, or Improve What You've Got.* New York: Paragon House, 1992.

Garner, John C. *Health Insurance Answer Book.* New York: Aspen Publishers, 1998.

Humber, Wilson J. *Buying Insurance: Maximum Protection at Minimum Cost.* Chicago: Moody Press, 1994.

Scott, David L. *The Guide to Buying Insurance.* Old Saybrook, Conn.: Globe Pequot Press, 1994.

Useful Addresses

American Insurance Association
1130 Connecticut Avenue NW
Washington, DC 20036

I.C.T. Insurance Consulting
2 Bloor Street West, Suite 100-538
Toronto, Ontario M4W 3E2
Canada

Independent Insurance Agents of America
127 South Peyton Street
Alexandria, VA 22314

Insurance Information Institute
110 William Street
New York, NY 10038

Internet Sites

Better Business Bureau
http://www.bbb.org

Consumer Insurance Guides
http://www.iiaany.com/constips.htm

Health Insurance Terms
http://www.jalden.com/Website/netdef.html

Insurance Canada
http://www.insurance-canada.ca/

Insurance News Network
http://www-002.connix.com/resources.html

Life Insurance Needs Calculator
http://www.1stquote.com/Insurance_Needs.htm

Index